DEGAS DANCERS

Le 'pas de deux' sur la scène
Oil on canvas: 1873–4: $24\frac{1}{4}'' \times 18\frac{1}{4}''$
(Home House Trustees, Courtauld Institute, London)
See also plate 14.

Edgar Degas

BALLET DANCERS

Selected with an Introduction by
Lillian Browse

The Folio Society
London 1960

PRINTED IN GREAT BRITAIN
Printed by Robert MacLehose & Co Ltd, Glasgow
Set in 'Monotype' Plantin
Bound by Richard Clay & Co Ltd, Bungay

Introduction

The great figures of Degas and Cézanne tower like giants over the second half of the nineteenth century in France, one of the most remarkable and prolific periods in the whole history of painting. The century which opened with Ingres as the protagonist of the Classical movement, which found two Romantic challengers in the persons of Delacroix and Géricault, which produced the traditional Corot as leader of the Barbizon School of landscapists as well as Courbet and Millet – respectively political and social rebels – reached its climax with the advent of the Impressionists and Expressionists and closed with Picasso and Braque at the outset of their careers.

The scene was so teeming with life and vigour, so many now famous names claimed attention, that a number of excellent painters were overlooked and did not begin to emerge until the second world war brought about the unprecedented art boom which made the first-range artists almost unattainable.

Now that the Impressionists have also slipped into the category of Old Masters, it is difficult to envisage the opposition with which their achievements were originally greeted. The shock was pertinently illustrated in a contemporary caricature wherein a pregnant woman, about to enter one of the Impressionist exhibitions, was gravely warned by the attendant that it might be more than unwise for her to pass through the turnstile.

It is also fascinating to reflect upon the various degrees of fame, inevitably gauged by market prices, of the painters whose names have now become household words. Renoir, with his charming nostalgic subjects, his 'easy-on-the-eye' canvases, was the first to lead in public favour. His priority has since been challenged by the Post-Impressionists, Gauguin, Van Gogh and Lautrec, and finally won from him by Cézanne, one of the clumsiest, most uncompromising and grandest artists of all time.

Apart from the fact that he had a great natural ability, the same may be said of Degas. The two men, although they exhibited in many of the Impressionist exhibitions, were certainly not Impressionists themselves. Both had an austere and highly intellectual approach towards their work; both embraced the tenets of sculpture in their chosen media, the one through his noble and enduring landscapes, the other through the timeless monumentality of the human form. The Impressionist discoveries about the play of light and the colour in shadows, the evanescent effect of dazzling illumination, were absorbed by Cézanne and Degas as a means and not used as an end. Their aims and achievements were more profound, their values more lasting, and therefore they stand apart as being in a class by themselves, two comets in a starry sky.

Subconsciously, no doubt, man finds it difficult to relinquish the standard of the idealistic human form as set for him by the Classical Greek masters, and to accept the kind of truth, relentlessly pursued and without any glorification, which was Degas' particular and original contribution. The accusations levelled against him of uncouth bodies, ugly clumsy women – supposedly the outcome of his proverbial dislike of the female sex, even now blind the majority to his superb achievements. And as his art rose with his age to its greatest heights, penetrating deeper and deeper beneath the surface and jettisoning all attractive superficialities, so it became more difficult for the average eye to grasp. It is for this reason, and no other, that Degas is by and large still underrated. But the pendulum is slowly swinging in his direction and it is certain that finally his gigantic stature will be fully recognised and valued among the greatest in art.

Hilaire-Germain-Edgar De Gas was born in Paris in 1834. He was one of a family of five, the children of Monsieur De Gas and his Creole wife, Mademoiselle Musson of New Orleans. De Gas *père* came from a rich French family who had a banking business in Naples and upon his marriage he settled in Paris where his children were born and educated.

Edgar Degas, the first to write his name thus, went to the Lycée Louis le Grand, and there he met Henri Rouart who was to become his oldest and dearest friend. From the Lycée he entered the Law School, as Monsieur De Gas envisaged a legal career for his eldest son. Before he was twenty, however, Edgar knew for a certainty that he was going to be a painter and with the support of Monsieur Valpinçon, an old family friend, he managed to persuade his father to allow him to enrol at the École des Beaux Arts.

In the home of the Valpinçons Edgar first saw and admired the drawings of Ingres, and at the École des Beaux Arts he worked under an obscure painter by the name of Louis Lamothe who had at least one distinction in the young student's eyes, that of having been a pupil of the grand old Classical master. But no art school ever seems able to hold a brilliant student for long, and as copying in the Louvre was part of the school's curriculum, Degas soon found that this side of his studies was far more suited to his tastes and temperament than the hours spent before *natures mortes* and models in the class room. Besides Ingres had said '*Il faut apprendre à peindre d'après les Maîtres et n'aborder la nature qu'après*', so that when Degas went on a visit to Italy in 1856 – to Naples, Florence and Rome, where he spent three years – he continued to make copies after the frescoes and drawings of the Italian masters. Besides these he painted a few canvases of Italian peasants and did some portrait-drawings and etchings. The Italian countryside, so lovingly embraced in the religious themes of the Renaissance painters, so nobly depicted by Claude and Poussin and so romantically by Richard Wilson, stirred him not at all. During the whole of his long working life Degas painted only two groups of *paysages*, a series of slight impressions, many in pastel, in the summer of 1869 and a smaller but more important group round about 1895, when he was spending a holiday at St Valéry-sur-Somme with his friend Braquaval.

The popular conception of Degas, the man, is that he was a misanthrope. Strictly speaking this was not true. While neither his temperament nor his passionate devotion to his art allowed him to be gregarious, he was devoted and loyal to his chosen circle putting himself to much trouble to help his friends should the necessity arise. Indeed one of his strongest characteristics was his loyalty to everything which touched him deeply, the kind of loyalty which might equally be called obstinacy. He had the unerring gift, even as a young man, of knowing exactly what he wanted and where he could best find it. At the age of twenty he was a disciple of Ingres, and notwithstanding his own stupendous achievements during the ensuing years, his admiration and respect were just as great when he died at the age of eighty-three. In the same way he remained constant to his life-long friends, his choice of subjects, his hatred of what is known as progress and his mistrust of internationalism, of which his much stressed anti-semitism was a form.

On his return to Paris, Degas continued to live with his parents, but worked in a studio on the left bank in the rue Madame. He began by painting large compositions on historical themes as well as his first theatrical subject, *Semiramis construisant une Ville*, a scene from the opera of that name. He also painted single portraits and portrait-groups including *Manet écoutant à sa femme au piano*. In 1860 Degas also painted *Le Départ*, his first racecourse scene, and two years later his *Course de Gentlemen avant le Départ* which, together with the portraits, were his first canvases of contemporary subjects. *Semiramis* was followed some six years later, in 1866, by another large canvas based upon a theatrical subject, *Mlle Fiocre dans le ballet 'Le Source'*. But apart from the knowledge that these two paintings were inspired by an actual 'set' seen by Degas in the theatre, they could easily be regarded as part of – and indeed belong to – the group of historical compositions. Their size, their somewhat self-conscious and careful planning, together with the frozen static poses of their figures, are reminiscent of the first essays. They give little hint of the brilliance and originality with which later Degas was to handle the theatre and its world, and therefore their importance is mainly historical.

As late as 1869 Degas was still disciplining himself by copying the old masters, Holbein, Poussin and, surprisingly enough, Lawrence, while he allowed himself little by little more freedom in his already remarkable portraits such as that of James Tissot and the portrait group – again in the theatre – *L'Orchestre de l'Opéra* which included the head of his friend the bassoonist, Désire Dihau (see also Plate 3). Besides its intrinsic qualities, *L'Orchestre de l'Opéra* is a most important picture in Degas' œuvre. Not only was it the first of the small series on the same theme – carefully rendered portrait groups of members of the orchestra and stalls with a background of dancers on the stage, but it also shows that Degas had really become fascinated by the possibilities of the theatre, a fascination which gradually led to his obsession with the dancers themselves.

In the early 'sixties, Degas met Manet. The friendship which sprang up between them was not surprising, for of all the members of the circle of the Café de la Bade and later of the Café Guerbois, these two young men had similar backgrounds both culturally and materially. Duranty, the critic, was also Degas' friend and social equal; Pissarro, Cézanne, Monet, Renoir, Sisley and Zola were all of humbler stock. Degas paid a visit to London with Manet in the summer of 1868. He also passed through Liverpool on his way to and from the States in 1872, but otherwise he never again came to England, for, a typical Parisian, he was nothing of a traveller. Despite his brief glances at this country he retained a lively and amused impression of the people and their customs, for in later years, when Sickert became one of his close friends and disciples, it delighted him to tease the English painter about the land of his adoption.

Even in his early years, Degas suffered from a defect in his right eye. On account of it he was transferred during the Franco-Prussian war from the infantry, in which he had enlisted, to an artillery regiment commanded by Henri Rouart. The freezing nights of that winter when he was on duty are said to have aggravated the trouble and made it chronic, and as the years progressed he suffered an ever-growing disability – one of the cruellest possible for a painter. Only his great strength of will and his dedication to his work enabled him, not only to rise above, but even to profit by it.

The trip to the United States seems to have been made on account of family business and also because Degas probably felt the need to give his eyes a rest after the hardships of the Siege of Paris. He went with his youngest brother, René, to his second brother's home in New Orleans. During this holiday he again painted family portraits.

On his return to Paris at the end of 1873 Degas found things considerably changed. The *Opéra* had been burned down during his absence and just as it was beginning to mean so much to him in his work. Many friends, having left the city during the siege, had settled in the country and, following the post-war boom, a serious slump had set in. His circle, the *peintres indépendants*, had not exhibited together for ten whole years, since the Salon des Refusés in 1863. Knowing from past experience that it was hopeless to submit their work to the official Salon and feeling it was time that they again made some concerted effort, they got together and launched the first Impressionist Exhibition in 1874. Altogether eight of these exhibitions were held, the last in 1886, and Degas not only participated in all but one, but he also acted as one of the chief organisers.

By 1886 he had reached his middle period, that is to say that he had roughly half his working life behind him. He had already established himself as a painter of very particular themes – racecourses, laundresses, milliners, women taking a tub, and above all dancers. His name has become so naturally linked with these completely original subjects that his not inconsiderable series of brilliant portraits is apt to be overlooked. True to his life-long insistence on the accidental he also aimed in his portraits at giving '*à leur figure le même choix d'expression qu'on donne à leur corps*', and that he absolutely achieved this object as well as the perfect and informative relationship between the sitter and his background, may be seen in such well-known portraits as *Carlo Pellegrini* in the Tate Gallery and *Duranty* in the Burrell Collection in Glasgow. Such canvases are not only masterpieces of portraiture, but they are also documents of human and social importance.

Like Constantin Guys and Lautrec in his early years, Degas was fascinated by the horse, so fashionable an animal in France during the reign of Napoleon III. To him it was not a symbol of pomp or bravery, the status it assumed in 17th century equestrian portraits; neither was it the snorting powerful creature of the Romantic compositions of Delacroix or Géricault. He did not see it like Stubbs as the old family friend and helpmeet, nor as the characterless means whereby a nation could fulfil its love of sport and gambling. Degas' horse is a wonderful creature in its own aesthetic right, a sensitive quivering mixture of muscular strength and nervous sensibility, an animal – like a ballet dancer – capable of an infinite variety of movements and disciplined to the last degree. Though he was far from being a 'horsey' man or race-goer, Degas found magnificent ready-made material at Longchamps and Chantilly. His astonishingly retentive memory – perhaps aided by snapshots, seized upon the unbelievable contortions of which a race-horse is capable as it dances restlessly before the 'tapes', its shiny coat damp with nervous sweat, its nostrils dilated, its head tossing in an almost unbearable pitch of excitement as it strains to be away. In the quietness of his studio Degas recorded his facts in numbers of masterly drawings and assembled them at his leisure in oil paint and pastel. He was strongly opposed to the practice of '*plein air*' painting and in any case it would have been an impossibility to set up an easel on the spot, and paint so fleeting a moment as the start of a race. The rapid oil-sketch was never his practice and there is no evidence that he even used quick sketches in a note book. His racecourse pictures are therefore almost as remarkable for the way in which they were achieved as for the results themselves, and apart from their great intrinsic qualities they have captured in lasting artistic statements those split seconds which otherwise have only been caught by a camera.

Degas' *Repasseuses* and *Modistes* and his great series of *Baigneuses*, link up naturally with the dancers. The first two groups are relatively small; the latter engrossed him nearly all the years of his maturity. The *Modistes* are lighter in vein and rather witty in mood, as if the artist were amusing himself by pandering to the foibles of the weaker sex. The *Repasseuses*, sometimes reminiscent of Daumier, are penetrating and objective human studies on a theme never before explored by a painter. The wide open movements of the women folding sheets, the pressure of the bodies forcing their weight on to the ironing table, and the tired moments of relaxation from heavy and monotonous work spelled a kind of beauty for Degas which was much after his own heart. Like the *rats de l'opéra*, these homely women were working at their *métier* not bothering about the painter who would send them down to posterity.

It seems impossible that any future painter will have the temerity ever to attempt ballet as his subject. Degas has surely said the last word on it and his magnificent results have truly earned him the copyright. He has performed the extraordinarily rare feat of satisfying two normally opposed categories of critics; those whose primary concern is with pictorial values and those – their profession being the subject in question – whose first and foremost demands are for technical truth. Thus he has definitely refuted the theory of incompatibility between factual accuracy and artistic expression. The artist's extraordinary ability to penetrate to the depths of his theme, to grasp at a glance the essentials which normally take a lifetime of study, has at no time been better conveyed than by Degas. The complicated, esoteric and highly superficial language of the ballet dancer was grasped by him to an astonishing degree; he might have spent his whole life in a class-room just as he might equally have spent it on a racecourse. Humanly it is rather appealing that Degas happened to be working at a time when ballet in France was at its lowest ebb, for his 'stars' bear no great names and their bodies, made heavy and coarse by faulty training, have their feet far too firmly on the ground and bear little resemblance to the ethereal and beautifully proportioned figures now associated with ballerinas and corps-de-ballet alike. Their obvious efforts at lightness and grace make them rather appealing than otherwise. The great Romantic era of ballet was at its height in 1834, the year in which Degas was born; in 1909, when Diaghilev brought his ballet to Paris, Degas was an old man approaching the state of almost complete blindness.

Degas saw his first operas and ballets in the Salle de la rue Le Peletier, the theatre which witnessed the rise and fall of the Romantic ballet, and which, meant only as a temporary home for the *Opéra*, lasted for more than half a century. Apart from his inherent love of music, Degas had friends whose professions tied them to the world of opera – the Halévy family of composers and dramatists, and Désiré Dihau, among them. Once the ballet had taken his fancy, they could have arranged for him to go 'behind the scenes' and evidently did, for Degas soon became a frequent visitor at the opera schools.

The daily practice and *répétitions* in the class-rooms intrigued him and earned his respect, so that little by little he became more absorbed in the preparations than in the finished spectacle itself. He learned that physically the dancer's is the most exacting of all professions; that daily, in the heat or cold, feeling fit or not, she must work for hours at the *barre*, at *adage* and *allegro* – *élévation*, *batterie*, *pirouettes*, *pointes* and *port-de bras*; that every part of her body needs attention until all can be co-ordinated, until technique becomes so perfected that it no longer requires conscious thought. Only at this moment can everything be devoted to artistry. Of all men Degas appreciated this to the full; his own life was, as a dancer's must be, one of complete dedication.

About 1872 Degas began his countless drawings of dancers which he did from life both in the class-room and in his own studio. They were used for canvases always painted in the quietness of his home and many are squared to scale for the subsequent painting and have comments relating to the technical pose or *pas* of the dancer. The drawing (Plate 4) is of a *danseuse* in exactly the same position, but seen from a different angle, as the one about to perform an *enchaînement* in the lovely little *Leçon de Danse* (Plate 1). The study of *Une Réligieuse* (Plate 2) relates to the paintings of *Robert le Diable* (Plate 3), which would appear to be the last of the series from the auditorium before Degas retired behind the scenes. These early drawings are Ingres-like and academic in the best sense of the word. They, and the early *Leçon de Danse*, with its tightness, quiet tonality, thin smooth pigment and meticulous care of detail, are even tender, a quality that can seldom be applied to Degas. The drawing of the dancer stretching (Plate 6) includes a detail of a point already mentioned, that of an incompetent performer whose feet are in the painful position of just not being *sur les pointes*.

The pastel study (Plate 8) which relates to the *Classe de Danse de M. Perrot* in the Louvre is particularly interesting in that it is one of the first glimpses of dancers in far from idealistic positions. Away from the limelights *les rats de l'Opéra* – as the young trainees were called – the *corps de ballet* and even the *étoiles* behaved as very ordinary human beings; if they had an itch, they scratched themselves; if they were tired, they yawned. Degas was accused of maliciousness because he drew and painted them at these moments, but he had a horror of the self-conscious pose which the presence of the painter or camera-man normally inspires in a model. His aim was to catch the sitter unawares as if one were 'peeping through a key-hole'. How lovely is the relationship between these *Deux Danseuses en Repos*, how flowing is the rhythmic design made by their torsos, arms and legs, and how beautifully placed are their dark heads against the lightness of the background. The painting of *La Classe de Danse de M. Perrot* itself combines all the attributes of the Impressionists with the more lasting qualities at which Degas aimed. It seizes a never-to-be-repeated moment, yet pins it down for all time, not only by its charm, its effect of light and shade and alluring colour, but also by the brilliance of its drawing, the originality of its composition and its penetrating human truths. Its understanding of the situation is so exact as to make it an important historical document, yet it retains at the same time everything which constitutes a great work of art.

In the autumn of 1873 the opera house in the rue Le Peletier was destroyed by fire with an enormous loss of material – musical instruments and scores, the *décors* for nearly its entire repertoire and just on six thousand costumes. Fortunately the fire broke out soon after midnight so that only one person lost his life. For one year the opera found another temporary home in the Salle Ventadour, then in January 1875 the Nouvel Opéra, whose foundation stone had been laid just on thirteen years before, opened its doors. This remarkable building, a complete little world built on an island site right in the heart of Paris, is the one designed by Garnier which stands today. From the time of its brilliant inauguration it became one of Degas' favourite haunts. He once said '*Vous voulez me décorer, c'est donc que vous voulez me faire plaisir, eh bien, donnez-moi mes libres entrées à l'Opéra ma vie durante.*' It is difficult to know whether to take Degas at his word or not, for surely so celebrated an artist would have been given a free pass for all his life.

Strangely enough there is only one painting of *Classes de Danse* which can definitely be said to have been done in *L'Académie de Musique et de Danse*, as Garnier's Nouvel Opéra was originally called. This is one done in the circular room at the top of the building which has round porthole-like windows; all the other class-rooms in the opera house are lit from skylights above. It would also seem that the well-known canvas *La Classe de Danse – Adage* (Plate 12) was painted from drawings made at the rue Le Peletier, for no such spiral staircase exists in the Nouvel Opéra.

Degas evidently had a special feeling for the *rats de l'Opéra*, so named because they were the waifs of the theatre, wearing other people's discarded and cut-down clothes and begging a few sous with which to buy sweets. They entered the Opéra between the ages of seven and eight years, came from poor families, and as there was neither time nor provision for their education, they grew into women ignorant of everything but the profession chosen for them by their families. Their thin and undeveloped little bodies were touchingly recorded by Degas in many drawings such as *Battements sur les Pointes à la Barre* (Plate 26) and *Danseuse Debout à l'Eventail* (Plate 38); that their ever-watchful mothers were allowed to accompany them to classes and rehearsals is obvious from *Préparation pour la Classe* (Plate 12), *L'Attente* (Plate 20), as well as *La Famille Mante* and *La répétition d'un Pas de Trois* (Plates 24 and 25).

As only a part of the dancers' practice takes place in the class-room Degas followed to watch rehearsals on the stage. *Répétition d'un Ballet sur la Scène* (Plate 14) is a typical example which led to an extension of the theme, the dancer at the great moment of facing her audience, of which *L'Étoile* (Plate 16) is one of the earliest and best known examples.

Degas was by this time exploring various media. With his insatiable curiosity, besides painting in oils, he was experimenting in pastel, monotype, and also in bronze. In his early years he handled oil paint smoothly and thinly – as Ingres had insisted – *comme une porte* – he worked with colours from which an excess of oil had been drained, with distemper and with gouache. Together with the Italian, Chialiva, who had studied the chemistry of colours, he discussed a way of setting pastel without impairing its fresh and sparkling quality. Chialiva invented a recipe which Degas used with great success; its secret died with the Italian in 1914 and has never been penetrated since.

It is not surprising that nearly all through his life Degas should have turned his attention to the problems of sculpture. Not only was it one more medium to explore, but as the weight and monumentality of the body in all its diverse positions and movements was his particular field of research, there is nothing more natural than that he should have essayed it in its most solid three-dimensional form. Neither is it an exaggeration to place his sculpture as the most revealing and intimate part of his *œuvre*. It was meant for his pleasure and information alone – never designated to leave his studio. He modelled in wax and built upon the most primitive armature because, as far as is known, he never learnt the technique of sculpture. He needed to find out everything for himself. The only piece of sculpture that Degas ever exhibited was the famous *Petite Danseuse de Quatorze Ans* (Plate 29). She was modelled, as all his sculpture, in wax, and Degas made the startling and bold innovation of dressing her in a white tarlatan *tutu*, satin shoes and tying her hair with a blue satin bow. Huysmans wrote, '*Le fait est que, du premier coup, M. Degas a culboté les traditions de la sculpture comme il a depuis longtemps secoué les conventions de la peinture. . . .*' When Degas died, a large number of wax models in varying states of decomposition filled his studio. He would never have them cast in bronze because, as he told Vollard, it was too much responsibility, they lasted for ever. His executors, however, selected seventy-three different models which were cast and allowed out into the world shortly after his death.

After 1886 Degas led a more and more monastic life. As a man he had always been a celibate and, apart from one fanciful story which appears to have no foundation, no hint of any emotional association with a woman creeps into his life's story. He more or less gave up exhibiting in 'the brothels that picture shows are' and, in the centre of Paris he lived, as Daniel Halévy wrote, '. . . like an alchemist of old times, surrounded by sketches, canvases, drawing boards, copper plates, lithographic stones, mixing bowls to try out new methods, all the materials of his art.' Having had sufficient money to form his own collection, nearly two hundred and fifty works including those by Cuyp, Corot, Delacroix, Pissarro, Cézanne, Forain, Gauguin and, of course, Ingres, were found in his studio after his death. Apart from his most intimate friends, these were all the company he needed. He concentrated his vision more and more and in refutation of the worldly Zola's criticism that he could not 'accept a man who shut himself up all his life to draw a ballet girl as ranking co-equal in dignity and power with Flaubert, Daudet and Goncourt', Degas wrote, 'That's my idea of genius, a man who finds a hand so lovely, so wonderful, so difficult to render, that he will shut himself up all his life, content to do nothing else but indicate fingernails'. Degas did precisely this. His pre-occupation was not simply with fingernails but with the whole human form. The massiveness and force of its inherent structure, whether in movement or repose, never ceased to be a wonder to him; the female figure, with its juxtaposition of softness and strength and not on account of any feminine attraction, were his sole interest.

As a painter, a maker of pictures, Degas had reached his height. He had become a superb draughtsman, a composer of great originality, a designer with a wonderful feeling for rhythmic movement and a colourist of daring. He had explored his particular subjects in so personal a way as to bar any subsequent painter from approaching them, and whilst he retained his link with the classical tradition, he was essentially an artist of his own time.

Then, coincident with his retirement, his art passed into a higher and more esoteric plane. As he withdrew from the world, solitary and independent of all but his own circle, so he refused to make even the slightest artistic concession. Drawing, in its own right, and upon the most exalted plane, became synonymous with modelling in the great series of figure studies, large in scale and tremendous in content, upon which he concentrated absolutely. Mystery of atmosphere, effects of light, feeling for texture and allure of colour, all were subordinated as, summing up, he stated with the greatest possible economy, his formal aim of synthesising plasticity and movement. His interest did not lie in arrested movement – the frozen gesture of a film suddenly stopped, nor in the split second between one off-balance position and the next, but in the continuous progression of a form passing from one attitude to another, so that all is told of what has gone before as well as what will follow.

The body as seen in ordinary everyday life performs a minimum of the feats and contortions of which it is capable – a miraculous piece of machinery which grows stiff and rusty through lack of exploitation. A dancer's actual instrument is her body, the medium through which she expresses her art; a woman taking a bath also twists herself into positions only to be seen by 'peeping through a key-hole', and as the one theme naturally links up with the other, they were the subjects that Degas finally chose for his rapt and undivided attention.

The logical development of a painter is to begin on a small, controlled and delicate scale and then, as he gains greater knowledge and with it, freedom, to enlarge his scale, to dispense with detail and to work with an ever increasing certainty of attack. Degas had an additional reason to develop this tendency, for his failing eyesight would not, in any case, have allowed him to continue with the charming precision of the earlier works. He drew on an almost unprecedented scale, not as cartoons for paintings as did the Renaissance masters, but as works of art in their own right. The two studies in *Deux Danseuses Nues Debout* (Plate 55) which relate to the sculpture *Danseuse en 'Quatrième' les Mains sur les Reins* (Plate 54) are nearly half as large again as the original model in wax; the pastel of the *Deux Danseuses se Dégourdissant à la Barre* (Plate 64) measures 50 × 43 ins. which approximates to a painting of no mean size.

Finally the *tutus* themselves were abolished as Degas reiterated his studies ever delving more deeply beneath the surface, and as the Nudes became increasingly more abstract, relating to the human body, but magnificently soaring above it, a lofty splendour, aloof and detached as the artist, manifested itself. This was the natural evolution of Degas' art, continuing its rise up to its grandest peak.

Degas died in a deserted Paris in September 1917. There were few friends left to attend his funeral and the great artist slipped away almost unnoticed by a war-racked people. His devoted friend and disciple, Forain, was one of the chief mourners. Degas had told him that he wanted no funeral oration, but '*Si, Forain, vous en ferez un, vous direz donc, "Il aimait beaucoup le dessin, moi aussi", et vous rentrez chez vous*'.

List of Plates

1 *La Leçon de danse*
Oil on panel: circa 1872: $7\frac{3}{4}'' \times 10\frac{5}{8}''$
(Metropolitan Museum of Art, New York)
In the opera-house, rue le Peletier: only the
violinist, not the *maître de danse* is seen.

2 *Une religieuse. Etude pour 'Robert le Diable'*
Peinture à l'essence: 1871–2: 17″ × 13¼″
(Victoria and Albert Museum, London)
See also plate 3.

3 *Le ballet de 'Robert le Diable'*
Oil on Canvas: 1874–6: 29¾″ × 32″
(Victoria and Albert Museum, London)
On extreme left M. Helch holding his glasses, may
be seen; behind him, Désiré Dihau, in profile; and
third from the right, with beard, le Vicomte Lepic.

4 *Danseuse en 'quatrième derrière, pointe tendue'*
Pencil and crayon, heightened with white chalk, on pink paper: circa 1872: $16\frac{1}{8}'' \times 11\frac{1}{4}''$
(Fogg Museum, Cambridge, Mass.)
In his early pictures, when he was only attempting dancers in static positions, Degas frequently
used this 'quatrième derrière', which is a preparatory position for 'enchainements'.

5 *Danseuse debout, vue de dos*
Pencil and chalk: circa 1872: size unknown
(Owner unknown)

6 *Danseuse se dégourdissant à la barre*
Charcoal heightened with white and pastel: circa 1875: 18″ × 12″
(Owner unknown)

7 *Danseuse assise*
Pencil and gouache on pink paper: circa 1872: $11\frac{1}{4}'' \times 9''$
(John Nicholas Brown, Providence)

8 *Deux danseuses en repos*
Pastel: 1874: $17\frac{1}{4}'' \times 11\frac{7}{8}''$
(Mr & Mrs J. Watson Webb, New York)
One of the earliest dancing subjects,
executed by Degas in pastel.

9 *La classe de danse de M. Perrot*
Oil on canvas: circa 1874–6: $33\frac{1}{4}'' \times 30\frac{1}{2}''$
(Mr Payne Bingham, New York)
One of the earliest pictures in which Degas
showed a dancer in the middle of a movement.

10 *Danseuse posant*
Charcoal heightened with white: 1878–9: 18″ × 11¼″
(Private owner in the U.S.A.)
A study for the painting reproduced as plate 23.

11 *Danseuses sur la scène avant la représentation*

Oil on silk: circa 1875–80: $6\frac{3}{8}'' \times 11\frac{5}{8}''$

(In a private collection)

It is evident that the above picture was originally designed by Degas as a fan, not only because it is painted on silk with the markings of the positions of the ribs visible, but also because the top left-hand corner clearly shows the original peripheral boundary.

12 *Préparation pour la classe*
Pastel: circa 1877: 24″ × 37″
(Glasgow Art Gallery and Museum)

13 *Deux danseuses debout, vis à vis*
Peinture à l'essence on pink paper: circa 1876: 24⅛″ × 15½″
(Metropolitan Museum of Art, New York)

14 *Répétition d'un ballet sur la scène*
Peinture à l'essence on paper, mounted on canvas: circa 1874–5: $21\frac{3}{8}'' \times 28\frac{3}{4}''$
(Metropolitan Museum of Art, New York)
The 'maître' in this picture is probably Eugène Coralli.

15 *Danseuse en blanc sur les pointes*
Pastel: 1873–4: $16\frac{1}{2}'' \times 11\frac{1}{2}''$
(Owner unknown)

16 *Danseuse sur la scène. 'L'Etoile'*
Pastel: circa 1876: 23″ × 17″
(Musée du Louvre, Paris)
One of the first pictures in which Degas
shows the dancer executing a *pas sauté*.
For another version see plate 53.

17 *La loge de danseuse*
Pastel: 1878–9: 24″ × 17″
(Oskar Reinhart, Winterthur)

18 *Danseuse rajustant sa chaussure. Melina Darde*
Charcoal heightened with white: 1878: $16\frac{1}{4}'' \times 12''$
(Owner unknown)
The name, Melina Darde, is quite unknown.
She was probably one of the *rats de l'opéra*.

19 *Danseuse assise. Melina Darde*
Charcoal heightened with white: circa 1878: 17″ × 12″
(Owner unknown)

20 *L'attente*
Pastel: circa 1879–80: 19″ × 24″
(Horace Havemeyer, New York)

21 *La classe de danse. 'Adage'*

Oil on canvas: circa 1876: $22\frac{1}{2}'' \times 32\frac{5}{8}''$ (Glasgow Art Gallery)

The 'maître de danse' in right distance is probably M. Pluque; the 'mère' with group of dancers on extreme right is Sabine Neyt, Degas' housekeeper. The classroom, like all those with long French windows, is in the opera-house rue Le Peletier.

22 *Danseuse bleue*

Oil on canvas: circa 1878–9: 13″ × 10″

(M. Ayard Vallotton, Lausanne)

The dancer stands with arms *en couronne* and left foot *sur la pointe
en quatrième devant* with bent knee. See also plate 23.

23 *Danseuse posant chez un photographe*
Oil on canvas: 1878–9: 26″ × 20″
(Museum of Modern and Western Art, Moscow)
See also plate 10

24 *La famille Mante*
Pastel: circa 1882: size unknown
(Owner unknown)
Suzanne Mante is the child being dressed by
Mme. Mante. Blanche Mante stands on left.

25 *La répétition dans la salle d'un 'pas de trois'*
Oil on canvas: circa 1880: 32″ × 29½″
(Pennsylvania Museum of Art)

battements sur les pointes à la barre

Degas

26 '*Battements sur les pointes à la barre*'
Charcoal on pink paper: circa 1883–5: size unknown
(Owner unknown)
The model is a child by the name of Dugés, and all Degas' drawings of her show the faults
that might be expected of a beginner, especially the *knobbly* knees whose muscles she has
not yet learned to draw up, the insteps not yet stretched and the *drooping* elbows.

27 *Pendant le repos*
Pastel: circa 1880–2: 29⅝″ × 21⅝″
(Owner unknown)

28 *Trois études de danseuse 'en quatrième'*
Charcoal heightened with pastel: circa 1878–80: 19″ × 24″
(Owner unknown)
Degas obviously did these studies in order to gain information
for his *petite Danseuse de Quatorze Ans*, plate 29.

29 *La Petite Danseuse de Quatorze Ans*

Bronze with tarlatan skirt and satin ribbon, on wooden base: 1880: height 39½″

It does not seem to be known how many copies of *La Petite Danseuse de Quatorze Ans* were cast; apart from the one belonging to Mr Sainsbury from which this photograph was taken, other casts are in the Musée du Louvre, the Virginia Museum of Fine Arts, and the Metropolitan Museum of Art, New York.

30 *Le repos. Deux danseuses assises*
Pastel: circa 1880–2: $19\frac{3}{4}'' \times 23''$
(Museum of Fine Arts, Boston, Mass.)

31 *Groupe de danseuses dans une salle*
Oil on canvas: circa 1880–2: $29\frac{1}{2}'' \times 29\frac{1}{2}''$
(Tate Gallery, London)

32 *Avant la représentation*
Oil on canvas: circa 1882–3: 19¼" × 25"
(The National Gallery of Scotland, Edinburgh – Maitland Bequest)

33 *Deux danseuses executant 'grands battements à la barre'*
Pastel: circa 1882–4: $25\frac{1}{4}'' \times 18\frac{3}{4}''$
(Mr & Mrs J. Watson Webb, New York)

34 *Deux danseuses derrière un portant*
Pastel and distemper: circa 1880: $27\frac{1}{2}'' \times 19''$
(Mrs Edward Jonas, New York)

35 *Deux études d'une danseuse debout*
Pastel and charcoal on green paper: circa 1878–80: $25\frac{1}{8}'' \times 19\frac{1}{4}''$
(Metropolitan Museum of Art, New York)
The pastel relates to the *La Petite Danseuse de Quatorze Ans,* and it would
seem as if Degas were contemplating doing the sculpture with this
different angle of the head and placing of the arms. See also plate 28.

36 *Avant la classe*
Pastel: circa 1882: $24\frac{1}{2}'' \times 18\frac{1}{2}''$
(Denver Art Museum, Colorado)
The old lady seen full-face seems to be
Degas' housekeeper, Sabine Neyt.

37 *Danseuses pendant le repos*
Pastel: circa 1880–3: $19'' \times 25\frac{1}{2}''$
(Owner unknown)

38 *Danseuse debout à l'éventail*
Pastel on green paper: circa 1883: 24″ × 16½″
(Metropolitan Museum of Art, New York)

39 *Danseuse attachant ses rubans*
Pastel: circa 1880: 25″ × 19″
(National Gallery of Victoria, Melbourne)

40 *Danseuse au bouquet derrière une femme à l'éventail*
Pastel: circa 1878–80: 16″ × 19¾″
(Museum of Art, Rhode Island School of Design)
For another picture on a similar theme see plate 42.

41 *Deux danseuses à mi-corps à l'éventail*
Pastel: circa 1883–5: $22\frac{1}{4}'' \times 32\frac{1}{4}''$
(Glasgow Art Gallery and Museum)

42 *Au théâtre, le ballet vu d'une loge*
Pastel: circa 1885: 24″ × 18″
(Private English Collection)

43 *Danseuses en scène*
Pastel: circa 1884–6: $25\frac{1}{2}'' \times 19\frac{1}{2}''$
(Mr & Mrs Frank H. Ginn, Cleveland)

44 *Danseuse saluante, un bouquet à la main*
Pastel: circa 1885 : 24″ × 18″
(Owner unknown)

45 *Danseuse verte vue de dos*
Pastel: circa 1884–6: 18″ × 12″
(Owner unknown)

46 *Danse espagnole*
Bronze: circa 1884: height 17″

47 *Danseuse nue en grande arabesque*
Bronze: circa 1882–6: height 16″

48 *'Porte de bras'. Danseuse vue de dos*
Sanguine: circa 1885: 12″ × 10″
(Owner unknown)

49 *Danseuse nue 'en quatrième devant'*
Bronze: circa 1882–90: height 22"

50 *Sur la scène. Danseuse verte*
Pastel: circa 1884–6: $24\frac{1}{2}'' \times 14''$
(Owner unknown)
As in Plates 42 and 43, strong emphasis is laid
upon the pattern made by arms and legs.

51 *Trois danseuses en ligne diagonale sur la scène*
Pastel: circa 1884–6: $24\frac{1}{2}'' \times 18\frac{1}{2}''$
(Private collection in Scotland)

52 *Danseuse rose se dégourdissant le cou-de-pied*
Pastel: circa 1885–8: $23\frac{1}{2}'' \times 17\frac{1}{2}''$
(Sam Salz, New York)

53 *Danseuse au bouquet*
Pastel worked over with oil paint: circa 1882–4: $26'' \times 14\frac{1}{2}''$
(Musée du Louvre)

54 *Danseuse en 'quatrième' les mains sur les reins*
Bronze: circa 1882–90: height 17¼″

55 *Deux danseuses nues debout*
Charcoal: circa 1900: $24'' \times 18\frac{1}{2}''$
(Owner unknown)

56 *Danseuse debout, les mains dans les emmanchures*
Black chalk heightened with pastel: circa 1885–90: 12″ × 10″
(Owner unknown)

57 *Danseuses à une répétition. Etude*
Charcoal heightened with pastel: circa 1888–90: 24″ × 19″
(Owner unknown)

58 *Quatre danseuses à mi-corps*
Charcoal or pastel: circa 1900: $26\frac{3}{8}'' \times 18\frac{3}{8}''$
(Owner unknown)

59 *Quatre danseuses bleues à mi-corps*
Pastel: circa 1900–5: $25\frac{1}{2}'' \times 26''$
(Museum of Modern and Western Art, Moscow)

60 *Danseuses debout sur la scène*
Pastel: circa 1905–12: $29\frac{1}{2}'' \times 22\frac{1}{2}''$
(Owner unknown)

61 *Le repos. Trois danseuses*
Oil on canvas: circa 1888–90: 20″ × 24½″
(Queensland Art Gallery, Brisbane)

62 *Trois danseuses, décor d'arbres*
Pastel: circa 1900–5: $19\frac{1}{2}'' \times 18''$
(Glasgow Art Gallery and Museum)

63 *Trois danseuses vues à mi-corps*
Pastel: circa 1900–12: 26″ × 20″
(Owner unknown)

64 *Deux danseuses se dégourdissant à la barre*
Pastel: circa 1900–5: 50″ × 43¼″
(National Gallery of Canada, Ottowa)

65 *Etude de trois danseuses aux bras levés*
Charcoal heightened with white: circa 1900: $18\frac{1}{2}'' \times 24''$
(Owner unknown)
See also plate 67.

66 *Quatre danseuses se reposant dans les coulisses*
Pastel: circa 1900–5: 28″ × 26″
(City Art Museum, St Louis, U.S.A.)

67 *Danseuses roses aux bras levés*
Pastel: circa 1900: $33\frac{1}{8}'' \times 22\frac{7}{8}''$
(Museum of Fine Arts, Boston, Mass.)

68 *Trois danseuses nues*
Charcoal: circa 1905–12: $34\frac{1}{2}'' \times 30\frac{1}{2}''$
(Owner unknown)

69 *Quatre danseuses nues*
Charcoal: circa 1905–12: $22\frac{1}{2}'' \times 19''$
(Owner unknown)

Acknowledgements

Photographs have very kindly been supplied by Archives photographique plates 16 and 53, John Nicholas Brown plate 7, The City Art Museum, St Louis plate 65, The Denver Art Museum plate 36, Durand Ruel, Paris plates 6, 20, 28, 37, 45, 48, 55, 57, 60, 63, 65, 68 and 69, The Fogg Museum plate 4, Knoedler & Co, London plates 27, 34, 44 and 58, Kunsthistorik Pladearkiv, Copenhagen plate 17, Leicester Galleries, London plates 10, 46 and 54, Metropolitan Museum of Art plates 9, 13, 14, 35 and 38, Museum of Fine Arts, Boston plates 30 and 67, National Gallery of Canada plate 64, National Gallery, London plate 47, National Gallery of Victoria plate 39, National Gallery, Stockholm plate 43, The Pennsylvania Museum of Art plate 25, Reid and Lefevre, London plate 50, S.C.R. London plates 23 and 59, Victoria and Albert Museum plates 2 and 3, Mr and Mrs Watson Webb, New York plates 8 and 33, Georges Wildenstein, New York plate 40, Sir Robert Witt Library, London plates 5 and 19.